WISE CRACKS

WISE CRACKS

by
SHYAM SINGHA

First published in Great Britain by

Cairns Publications
47 Firth Park Avenue
Sheffield
S5 6HF

In association with

John Hunt Publishing Ltd.
46A West Street
New Alresford
Hants.
SO24 9AU

ISBN 1 903019 19 2

A CIP catalogue record for this book is available from the
British Library.

Printed in Malta by Interprint Ltd.

Everything is not that good,
and part of it is excellent

*A*bsence makes the heart go yonder.

*A*ccidents happen only in a well regulated chaos.

*A*dam's ale is vodka, and a little water.

*A*dvice is never heeded when given but not needed.

*A*fter a storm there are more storms.

A good cock never gets caught.

*A*ll is lost when mind is frost.

*A*ll roads do not lead to Rome - try it.

'*A*ny port in a storm' is for cowards.

*A*s well be hanged for nothing - it happens every day.

*B*ad news does not travel, it explodes.

A bad workman drools over
his tools.

*T*he beaten road is for unimaginative
travellers.

*B*est is an opinion, not a truth.

*B*est is the cheapest, but beware of the
labels.

*B*etter be a stool than a hunting stick.

*B*etter be never sure lest you kill.

*B*etter bend than break - then you can have your cake.

*B*etter late than ever arriving.

*B*etter the devil you know than the angel you don't know.

A bird should be in a cage before you go round the bush.

*B*irds of a feather fight together.

*B*lack is beautiful because you can't change the colour.

*B*lessed are those who expect nothing, do nothing, and live the moment.

*B*low your trumpet in an open space.

*B*ooks and friends should be few but good and totally understood.

A bull is dangerous when taken by horns!

*C*all no man happy 'til he moves feet first.

*C*aveat emptor or Emperor.

*C*hanging human nature is harder than changing rivers and mountains.

*C*hildren should always be seen and
heard.

*C*hoosing is out when boozing
is in.

*C*leanliness is the only godliness.

*C*lothes removed makes the
gentleman a man.

*C*onmen are near relatives.

*C*onstant quest is no guest.

A contented mind is that of a cabbage.

*C*ourage and courtesy conquer cowardice.

*T*he course of true love has to run one month.

A cowl is a cover for monks' scowls.

A creaking gate lingers longer.

C rocodiles have no tear ducts.

D ead men leave no footsteps,
    only trails.

D eath revels in equality.

D eath sends its challenge in a grey
    hair.

*D*esires are never fulfilled, needs are.

*D*o as most do and you will
remain obscure.

*D*o as others say and you are
in trouble.

*D*o put new wine in old
bottles - it fetches more.

*D*o put a cart before the horse. It
shows imagination.

*D*o ride a high horse if you want to get noticed.

*D*o wash your dirty linen in public. It is political.

*D*on't cross a bridge with a mob.

*E*ager beavers sometimes drown.

*E*agles and owls have no goggles.

'*E*arly to bed, early to rise' shows you're still poor.

*E*ast or west, best is your own nest.

*E*at at pleasure, drink by measure.

*E*avesdroppers always come a cropper.

*E*ndowment is a policy of crooks.

*E*nough is half hunger in a feast.

*E*vil is that which looks good for
the moment.

*E*xorcise the habit, not exercise it.

*E*xperience is monotonous
repetition.

*F*irst thrive and then endless strive.

*F*ools never flourish with
fortunes.

*F*ootprints on the sands of time
should be erased.

*F*orced kindness is that of an
ugly ego.

*F*orward goes only who knows
backwards.

*F*owl, fame and fortunes soon fly
  away.

*F*riendship grows when you
  water it often.

*F*riendship is a sign of fitness.

*F*riendship is lost when you
  lend money.

*G*ive a dog a bad name and it
  will bite.

*G*ive a lie twenty-four hours and it will be a truth.

*G*ive and spend and God will send.

*G*ive credit only once.

*G*ive the devil no dues.

*G*luttony is a disease of suppression.

God always sends nuts to nutters.

God does nothing, the devil does it all.

God is never on any side of a war.

God need not help those who help themselves.

Good for the liver may be bad for the spleen.

Good heart seldom lies.

Gossiping and lying are cousins.

Grapes are sour for those who can't reach them.

Greatest talkers are swindlers.

Great men and women have great faults.

*G*reedy eaters dig their graves with
their teeth.

*G*reed always breeds cheating.

*H*abits are at first cobwebs, at
last cables.

*H*appy are those who have no
past lingering.

*H*appy is she who marries the son of
a dead mother.

*H*aste is the sister of repentance.

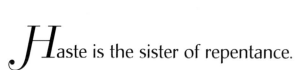

*H*ealth is better than sickly
 wealth.

A heavy purse is a curse of meanness.

*T*he highest can topple fastest.

*H*onesty is the best policy for the
 honest, not for a crook.

*H*ope for the best, and let the
    heart rest.

*I*dle folk have no sense of time.

*I*f a doctor cures, the sun sees it; if he
    kills, the earth hides it.

*I*f a little is good, more is
    not better.

*I*f a thing is worth doing, don't do it.

*I*f my ancestors had not died, I would have an army.

*I*f there were no clouds, we should have no rain.

*I*f you are a gladiator, quit Rome.

*I*f you are alive it means you did not die.

*I*f you are down you need fear no fall.

*I*f you begin many things you rarely finish any.

*I*f you do, you are in trouble, if you don't, the same.

*I*f you leave your house in search of happiness you pursue a shadow.

*I*f you make no mistakes you learn nothing.

*I*f you peep through a hole you may crick your neck.

*I*f you run after two hares you are a vegetarian.

*I*f you say what you like you shall hear what you do not like.

*I*f you sing before breakfast, you will do so till supper.

*I*f you want a thing done well learn to delegate well.

*I*f you will not when you may, later on you have no say.

*I*f you would eat the kernel you must crack the nut.

*I*f you would climb the ladder first find one.

*I*fs and buts drive us all nuts.

*I*n wine there is a swine who spills truth.

*I*t is as well to know who is blowing the trumpet.

*I*t is love that foolishly drowns people.

*I*t is useful to flog a dead horse. It takes the anger out.

*J*og your memory and you will find skeletons in the cupboard.

*J*uggling is the main principle of politics and law.

*K*ick a pillar and lose a toe.

*K*ill the goose that lays the golden eggs. It is a fake.

*K*ind hearts kindle warmth in others.

*K*ings and queens are now only in a pack of cards.

*K*naves can survive where knights do not.

*K*nowledge is power; too much knowledge is cowardice.

*K*nowledge, if real, creates mirth and laughter.

*K*nowing your faults is better than pointing out the faults of others.

*T*he last straw does not break the camel's back, rather it is the greed of the loader.

*L*ate comers are never bored.

*L*augh and put on some weight.

*L*augh and the world laughs with you?
No so any more. Laugh and they
lock you up.

*L*aw and justice have no
relationship.

*L*aws are made to stop loopholes in
previous laws.

*L*aws catch flies but let hornets
go free.

*L*eopards change spots to cheat.

*L*iars have good memories.

A light purse always uses
plastic money.

*L*ive, learn - then love, not before.

*L*ive not to eat, but eat to
live healthily.

*L*ove lacks loyalty in midsummer.

*L*ove speaks without speaking, but in the eyes.

*M*ake hay while the sun shines' - and get sunstroke.

A man is as old as he feels, and a woman - never ask.

*M*any hands for light work always creates problems.

*M*arriage is a potty lottery, where some win.

*M*ay God defend me from my friends - the devil will take care of my enemies.

*M*oney is not essential, but if you have some you can be uncomfortable in comfort.

*M*ore haste, more waste.

*M*ore people know you than you know.

*M*ost uncommon is common sense.

*N*ecessity is not the mother but the
motivator of invention.

*N*ever borrow or lend, just give
and take.

*N*ever look a gift horse in the mouth,
only hooves and tail.

'*N*ever put off 'til tomorrow what
may be done today' is a
disease called workaholism.

*N*ever spend your money before you
have it, otherwise it will
bankrupt bankers.

*N*eurotics build castles in the air,
psychotics live in them and
psychiatrists charge the rent.

*N*ew brooms are a fashion for a
clean sweep.

*N*inety-nine percent of inspiration is
determination.

*N*o one is infallible or indelible.

*O*ld age is a hospital that takes in
all diseases.

*O*ne of these days is a myth.

*O*nly fools can rush in - and sometimes win.

*O*nly the wearer knows where the shoe pinches, but others can see the limp.

*O*pen confession is good for the soul, but not for a spy.

*O*pportunities always knock, but not for the deaf.

*O*ut of debt is a myth in a plastic card society.

***

*P*addle your own canoe and you are in a muddle.

***

*P*atience was a virtue before the instant coffee era.

***

'*T*he pen is mightier than the sword' was true when postal deliveries were regular.

***

*P*itchers do not go to the well – tap water comes to the pitcher.

'A place for everything, and everything
in its place' is Victorian slang.

Pleasant hours do not tick on
a clock.

The pot has to call the kettle black. It is
a custom of all unions.

Pouring oil on the fire is a
political way of doing things.

Poverty is no sin. To say it is to
encourage poverty.

*P*ractice makes perfect repeating robots.

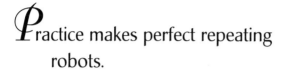

*P*ractise what you do not preach.

*P*raise is pleasant for a peasant but not for a priest.

*P*raise makes good people better and bad people worse.

*P*rocrastination is the game of politicians.

*T*he proof of the pudding is in the aroma.

*P*unctuality is forced on workers by the unpunctual bureaucrats.

*Q*uotas are created to hoard things.

*Q*uestions create more questions.

*R*ats desert a sinking ship because they can't swim.

*R*eal things always have shadows.

*R*elations, religions, rules are
ruled by heresy.

A remedy may cause worse disease,
but the prescriber will
prescribe another remedy.

*R*espect and familiarity are not
cousins.

*R*evenge is sweet when you are bitter.

*R*evenge never repairs an injury, but creates one more.

*R*ings are a sign of slavery.

A rolling stone gathers no moss but creates a lot of fun and floss.

*R*ugs are for comfort, not for pushing dirt under.

*R*unning away is no solution to a standing problem.

Sadness and gladness are faces of the same coin.

Safety lies nowhere but in the moment.

Second thoughts are trouble-makers.

'Seeing is believing' is an old joke.

Self-preservation is the poison of a materialistic society.

*T*he shortest way is a myth.

*S*ilence and solitude is the nest
of thought.

*S*ilence is effervescent bubbling.

*S*ilence may look golden but is
sometimes mean.

*S*ilence never makes mistakes.

Sleep is better than medicine.

A slow whirlwind is no good to a windmill.

A soft answer sows seeds of tranquillity.

Some are wise and some are totally otherwise.

Soon gotten soon forgotten.

*S*orrow is born of excessive joy.

A stitch in time saves twine
and time.

*S*ubmitting to one wrong multiplies it
further.

*S*uperstitions are born of fears.

*T*o take the bull by the horns you need
a red cloth.

*T*ake the rough and the smooth will follow.

A tale never loses in telling but gains magnitude.

*T*alk of the devil vividly, so that he disappears.

*T*he black sheep in the flock always stands out.

*T*he one who pays the piper rules the stage.

There is honour among thieves, but more among politicians.

There are three sides to every question. The third is silent.

There's always pleasure in pain and vice versa.

There's many a true word spoken in jest, just as a good craftsman may not pass a written test.

There's no place like home, only when you are far, far away.

'There is no rose without a thorn' is a myth. See the hybrid velvet one.

They who stand and wait are the winners.

'A thing of beauty is a joy forever' only for a connoisseur.

Things are always what they seem, but we seldom look at them.

Things done cannot be undone is wrong: ask any political party.

*T*hose who live in glass houses should
have them covered with a steel
mesh before throwing any stones.

*T*hrough hardship to the stars –
or to stomach ache.

'*T*hrough obedience learn to command'
is a fallacy – ask any junior clerk.

*T*ime and tide wait for the one
person who is totally ready.

*T*ime works wonders, because
you forget.

*T*o err is human, but to err again and
again is folly.

*T*omorrow never comes because
it does not exist.

*T*he tongue is not steel yet it cuts
and peels.

*T*oo many cooks spoil the broth
if any is left.

*T*ravel makes the wise better but the foolish worse.

*T*ruth is not God's daughter, but mother.

*T*wo dogs fight for a bone and the third takes it.

*U*neasy lies the head that wears a crown, either of thorns or of diamonds.

*U*nited we stand, only on a bandwagon.

*U*nused legs need crutches after a while.

*V*ictory is short, defeat lasts.

'*W*ake not a sleeping lion' is wrong - where else will you get courage from?

'*W*alls have ears' is wrong - nowadays it has bugs.

*W*ars bring scars.

'*T*he way to a man's heart is through his stomach' cannot be right in an era of TV dinners.

*W*e are all slaves of opinionated opinions.

*W*e soon believe what we desire – then force it on others.

*W*eak men strut like peacocks.

*W*ealth infatuates as much as beauty does.

*W*edlock is a padlock without a key.

*W*hat is a workman with or without his tools if he has no work?

*W*hat is felt in the bones is the gut feeling.

*W*hat is worth doing is worth waiting to know if it is worth doing.

*W*hat may be done at any time
is done in no time.

*W*hat must be must be' is the fatalistic
approach to life of a non-believer.

*W*hat soberness conceals, drunkenness
reveals, but awareness heals.

*W*hat the eye doesn't see but
thinks of seeing creates all the
heartaches of the world.

*W*hatever you sow, time and patience
is required for it to grow.

When children stand quiet
grown ups are suspicious.

When everybody is speaking there is
a buzzing hum and no listening.

When in doubt stay in doubt and
there will be no court cases.

When the cat is away mice sing
and sway.

When the wolf is at the door, do not
ask if he is a vegetarian.

*W*hen the word is out, ten tentacles it will sprout.

*W*hen thieves fall out, the city becomes safe.

*W*here ignorance is bliss it is mad folly to lose it.

*W*here there's a will, there are relatives.

*W*hile there is life, there is strife.

Who chatters is not interested in my matters.

❦

Who travels fastest travels alone.

❦

The wise are always alone, even in company.

❦

Wonder lasts not nine days but nine seconds.

❦

Words spoken are recorded in the cosmos.

*Y*ou are known by the company you refuse.

*Y*ou can burn the candle at both ends - as long as it is horizontal.

*Y*ou can have your cake and eat it if nobody is watching.

*Y*ou cannot have it both ways, only politicians have this prerogative.